Diet

The Ketogenic Diet Beginner's Bible

Ketogenic - Low Carb - Weight Loss Recipe Book

- 50 Delicious Recipes For Fat Loss -

Darrell White

© 2015

monetary loss due to the information herein, either directly or indirectly.

Respective authors own all copyrights not held by the publisher.

The information herein is offered for informational purposes solely, and is universal as so. The presentation of the information is without contract or any type of guarantee assurance.

The trademarks that are used are without any consent, and the publication of the trademark is without permission or backing by the trademark owner. All trademarks and brands within this book are for clarifying purposes only and are the owned by the owners themselves, not affiliated with this document.

My Free Gift To You!

As a way of saying thank you for downloading my book, I'd like to send you an exclusive gift that will revolutionize the way you learn new languages. It's an extremely comprehensive PDF with all the information you need know to provide you with 365-days-of-motivation.

This guide is an amazing complement to the book you just got, and could easily be a stand-alone product, but for now I've decided to give it away for free, to thank you for being such an awesome reader, and to make sure I give you all the value that I can to help you succeed faster on your language journey.

To get your FREE gift, go to the link below, follow the steps, and I'll send it to your email address right away.

TABLE OF CONTENTS

INTRODUCTION

Are you still shopping around for the best diet program for you? Have you tried lots of different diet programs in the past and none of them seem to work? Look no more because with Ketogenic Diet, you might get the diet you've been looking for with great results and less of the stressful eating habits associated with the not-so-helpful programs and recipes. Get ready for healthy and delicious recipes that will help you shed a pound a day!

The ketogenic diet is a high-fat, adequate-protein, low-carbohydrate diet that in medicine is used primarily to treat difficult-to-control (refractory) epilepsy in children. The diet forces the body to burn fats rather than carbohydrates. Fathers, we need you.

CHAPTER 1: THE KETOGENIC DIET

WHAT EXACTLY IS KETOGENIC DIET?

Definition - The Ketogenic Diet is your complete guide to understanding the right kind of food to consume and in the right proportions. This guide is equipped with a roadmap that teaches you how to choose the foods that give you the most vitamins and the most energy. The Ketogenic Diet is your way to:

Experience lots of energy and more willpower than you had before.

Shed off weight without being subjected to cravings and without being hungry.

Have your brain function at its best every day.

CHAPTER 2: HOW TO LOSE 1 POUND A DAY

GENERAL PRINCIPLE OF LOSING 1 POUND A DAY

Basically, the way to lose 1 pound per day is to shed 3500 calories a day. There are many tips and hacks that promise you an easy way of losing this pound but it's not that simple to burn through 3500 calories a day. Most people don't realize that the more weight you lose, the more successful you become in this 1-pound-a-day diet. When a person is closer to his body weight, the body holds on to its stored fat more and sacrifices muscle over fat. This doesn't mean, though, that you cannot achieve losing 1 pound per day, it just means that as you lose weight and become fitter, it will take more work to continue losing that amount of calories.

What you can do, once you're closer to your BMI, is to try losing 300-500 fewer calories per day in order to continue losing weight until you get the body you always wanted. Try not to be too hard on yourself and take it 1 day at a time using the right kind of foods. These are mostly Paleo-friendly foods or caveman foods. This is due to the fact that you'll be more successful in losing weight when you eat organic, non-processed, and natural foods.

CHAPTER 3: THE KETOGENIC DIET

SHOPPING LIST

In order to lose a pound a day and still adhere to The Ketogenic Diet's kinds of foods, here's a list of the specific foods that you should choose when you're out doing your grocery shopping.

Oils and Fats

— Tallow

— Ghee

— Butter

— Duck fat

— Coconut oil

— MCT oil

— Red palm oil

— Avocado oil

— Macadamia nut oil

— Olive oil

Vegetables

— Bok choy

— Asparagus

— Mushrooms

— Cabbage

— Garlic

— Squash (examples include butternut, spaghetti, etc)

— Cucumber

— Broccoli

— Kale

— Onion

— Cauliflower

— Avocado

— Artichokes hearts

— Cabbage

— Peppers (e.g. bell, banana and jalapeno, etc)

— Brussel sprouts

— Leafy greens (e.g. romaine, bib lettuce, spinach and arugula, etc)

— Spinach

— Lettuce

— Green onion

— Parsley root

— Water chestnuts

— Nightshades (e.g. tomatoes, eggplant and peppers)

Dairy

— Grass-fed butter

— Ghee

— Cream

— Full-fat cheeses

— Full-fat raw yogurt

— Butter (with the exception of margarines)

— Eggs

Sugar and Sweeteners

— Stevia

— Erythritol

— Xylitol

— Splenda

— Other sugar alcohol sweeteners

— Swerve

Condiments and Dressings

— Mustard with exception of sweetened mustards

— Lime juice

— Mayo

— Hot sauce

— Salsa

— Soy sauce (if you prefer gluten-free then you can opt for tamari)

— Lemon juice

— Ranch

— Mayonnaise

— Salad dressings (e.g. Caesar, Italian, Bleu Cheese, etc)

— Olives

— Cider and wine vinegars (if you decide to use balsamic vinegar then do so sparingly)

— beef sticks or beef jerky

— Most salsas

— Capers

— Pork rinds (the crushed ones can substitute bread crumbs)

— Vegetable stock or chicken stock

Proteins

— Eggs

— Ground beef

— Bacon

— Pasture-raised eggs

— Chicken (you can use the thighs, breasts and wings)

— Salami

— Ham

— Steak

— Pepperoni

— Pork or beef ribs

— Prosciutto

— Pork or beef roasts

— Deli cold cuts

— Pork chops or Loin

— Sausage

— Any kind of fresh or frozen fish (salmon, tuna, tilapia, cod and etc)

— Whey isolate

— Summer flounder

— Pastured-raised pork

Fruits

— Olives

— Blackberries

— Raspberries

— Cranberries

— Avocados

— Limes

— Mulberries

— Strawberries

— Rhubarb

— Coconuts

— Pomegranates

— Olives

— Blueberries

— Grapefruits

Nuts and Seeds

— Almonds

— Walnuts

— Hazelnuts

— Pumpkin

— Pistachios

— Pecans

— Sesame

— Macadamias

— Flax

— Sunflower

— Cashew nuts

— Chestnuts

Starches

— Carrot

— Yam

— Sweet potato

— Pumpkin

— Wild rice

— White rice

— Brown rice

— Cassava

— Banana

— Plantain

— Black rice

— Taro

— Butternut squash

Others

— Nut butters

— Herbs

— Unsweetened almond milk

— Pickles

— Almond flour / Almond meal

— Unsweetened cocoa powder

Shopping Tips for the Ketogenic Shopper

The main goal is to purchase grass-fed meat and wild-caught fish.

- To avoid impulsive buying and reduce impulses to buy junk food, you should shop when you're considerably full and not hungry.
- Try to look for products found around the perimeter of the store where most Ketogenic products are stored.
- Try asking a friend to go shopping with you. You'll have a second opinion on the stuff you buy.
- If you're not sure of the food you picked up, better not buy it at all.
- Try buying food online to save time and gas.
- It's cheaper and healthier to shop at your local farmer's market.

Chapter 4 The Ketogenic Diet Cookbook

Easy Recipes to make you lose 1 pound daily

Red Healthy Smoothie (serves 24 oz.)

Ingredients:

Half red bell pepper

1 red cabbage, chopped

1 Roma tomato

Half cup of raspberries

8 ounces of cold water

5 strawberries, medium-sized

1 square of ice cube, optional

Instructions:

Put all the ingredients in the blender. Make sure they will all fit and would not spill on the sides.

Put the cover tightly and blend on high. Make sure all ingredients are incorporated.

Serve chilled.

CREAMY CHOCOLATE MILK

This can make a great breakfast or you can take it as dessert after having your meal. It can make two servings.

Ingredients:

4 ounces of heavy cream

Unsweetened almond milk, 16 ounces

Crushed ice, ½ cup (this is optional and use it if you want the drink to be thick. However, you have to know that it will have a less intense flavor)

Artificial sweetener, 1 packet

Whey chocolate isolate powder, 1 scoop

Instructions

Place all the ingredients inside a blender and blend until the mixture becomes smooth.

You can make double this recipe because this smoothie is low carb and will still help you maintain the Ketogenic diet.

AVOCADO BLUEBERRY SMOOTHIE (SERVES 2)

Ingredients:

A cup of blueberries

A diced and cored apple

Half of a ripe avocado

A cup of coconut milk or water

A cup of crushed ice

A tablespoon of coconut oil

Half cup of plain, full fat yoghurt

A tablespoon of almond butter

Instructions:

Blend all ingredients in the blender until smooth and creamy. It's best served chilled.

Cucumber Spinach Smoothie

This is a great way of combining the delicious flavors that cucumber and spinach have. This shake is not only refreshing but crisp too. You can prepare it in less than 5 minutes and it can serve one person.

Ingredients

7 ice cubes

Spinach, 2 handfuls

MCT oil, 1-2 tablespoons

Liquid stevia, 12 drops

Peeled and cubed cucumber, 2.5 oz

Xanthan gum, ¼ tablespoon

Coconut milk, 1 cup (it's advisable to use the ones from cartons)

Instructions

Put the spinach and ice cubes in the blender. Add the coconut milk, stevia, MCT oil and Xanthan gum. Finally add the cucumber on top after peeling and cubing it.

Blend this mixture for about 1-2 minutes or until you are sure that the ingredients have been properly mixed. There will still be some bits of spinach in the smoothie but don't worry about them because you won't be able to taste them due to the texture.

Your smoothie is ready so you can pour it in your glass and enjoy.

KALE AND CHERRY SMOOTHIE

Ingredients:

A cup of frozen cherries or fresh ones and remove the pits

A cup of chopped kale leaves

A cup of orange juice, freshly squeezed

A cup of ice

1 tablespoons of raw coconut oil

2 tablespoons of hemp seed

Instructions:

Blend all ingredients together in the blender and mix until fully incorporated. Make sure it is completely smooth and serve cold.

Coconut Peach Paleo Smoothie

Ingredients:

A cup full of chilled fat coconut milk

2 large-sized, fresh and peeled peaches cut into chunks

A cup of ice

Fresh zest of lemon, for taste

Instructions:

Put the peaches, coconut mix, and ice to the blender.

Add a few gratings of lemon zest.

Blend until smooth and fully mixed.

Macadamia, Coconut, and Cocoa Smoothie

Ingredients:

A quarter cup of coconut milk, unsweetened (170 g)

2 tablespoons of "swerve" or other sugar equivalent (25g)

2 tablespoons of crushed macadamia nuts, salted (14g)

1 tablespoon of cocoa powder, unsweetened (5.40 g)

Half teaspoon of vanilla extract

A cup of ice cubes (180g)

A dash of salt

Instructions:

Pour all ingredients in a blender and blend until smooth and fully mixed.

Add whipped coconut cream, more macadamia nuts, and toasted coconut.

Serve chilled.

Spinach Smoothie with Lime, Apple, and Orange

Ingredients:

An orange

An apple

2 cups of spinach

Half slice of peeled lime

An inch of frozen ginger

A cup of ice cubes

A cup of almond milk

Instructions:

Peel the lemon and remove the core from the apple.

Grate the frozen ginger.

Put all ingredients in a blender and blend in high.

Make sure all ingredients are mixed and smooth.

Serve chilled.

CRANBERRY AND PUMPKIN- CREAMY AND DAIRY FREE (SERVES 1-2)

Ingredients:

A cup of non-dairy milk

¼ cup of fresh cranberries, frozen

¾ tsp. of cinnamon

¼ cup of soaked cashews, raw (use an equal amount of plain Greek yogurt if you don't want to add nuts)

2 tablespoons of coconut cream or coconut butter

A small apple, chopped into chunks

Half cup of fresh pumpkin puree

Half of a peeled orange

Instructions:

Put all ingredients in a blender and blend until smooth and creamy. Serve chilled.

Avocado Smoothie

This smoothie is a favorite of many people and you can also try it out.

Ingredients

5 tablespoons of avocado

½ cup of coconut milk

3 egg yolks

½ cup of water

Juice obtained from either lemon or lime

¼ cup of ice

Instructions

Mix all the ingredients inside a mixer and let it run until all the ingredients are properly mixed.

Your smoothie is ready and you can take it as it is.

You can also choose to use the ice can in order to give it that extra feeling.

FAT BOMB SMOOTHIE

This is one of the tastiest smoothies you can ever make. You can skip the extra salt included in the ingredients if you wish. However, if you feel like your salt intake is low then it is advisable to include it. It will help the other flavors to come out strongly too. In order to get a variation of this smoothie, you can include the various kinds of berries allowed on the Ketogenic diet (e.g. blue berries).

Ingredients

1/3 cup of strawberries

1 cup of coconut milk

A pinch of salt

2 tablespoons of coconut milk (unrefined)

Instructions

Mix all the ingredients inside a blend and blend until all the ingredients are properly mixed.

You can now have your smoothie.

APPLE PIE SMOOTHIE

Ingredients:

A medium-sized apple, peeled and cored (cut them into chunks)

¼ teaspoon of vanilla extract

Half cup of water (120 ml), you can also use yogurt

¼ teaspoon of ground cinnamon

A teaspoon of maple syrup

A pinch of nutmeg and all spice

A scoop of protein powder (optional)

Instructions:

Put the water, apple, vanilla, spices, and maple syrup in a blender and blend until fully mixed and smooth.

Put in a mug and heat in the microwave for 2 minutes.

Add cinnamon on top and serve.

WINTER SUNSHINE SMOOTHIE

Ingredients:

2 peeled oranges

Meat from a young Thai coconut

A cup of ice

A cup of reserved coconut water, add more if needed

2 tablespoons of goji berries

¼ cup of hemp seeds

¼ cup beet kvass, better if homemade

¼ teaspoon of turmeric

Instructions:

Put all the ingredients in the blender and blend until smooth and creamy.

Add in the beet kvass and continue blending.

KETO TROPICAL SMOOTHIE

Here is a Keto smoothie you can enjoy before the end of summer. This smoothie is a combination of various delicious fruity flavors. Although you are not supposed to take in too much colorful fruits and flavor when on a Ketogenic diet, you can find a way around it that will leave you with a delicious and healthy smoothie.

For this particular recipe, you can substitute almond milk with coconut milk if you wish. However, you should know that almond milk is normally more watery and so the smoothie may be less thick. This can make one serving.

Ingredients

½ tablespoon of mango extract

7 ice cubes

1 tablespoon of MCT oil

20 drops of Liquid stevia

¼ cup of sour cream

¾ cup of coconut milk (unsweetened)

¼ tablespoon of blueberry extract

2 tablespoons of flaxseed meal

Instructions

Put all the ingredients in the blender and give it some time in order for the flax meal to absorb some of the moisture.

Start blending until you get a thick consistency. This should take about 1-2 minutes.

Your smoothie is ready and you can now enjoy it especially on a hot day.

THE KETOGENIC COFFEE

Ingredients:

A cup of coffee that is freshly brewed, (8 to 12 oz)

A tablespoon of butter, unsalted and grass-fed

A tablespoon of coconut oil, MCT

Instructions:

Put the MCT oil and butter with the coffee in the blender and blend until creamy and make sure there is no oil sitting on its surface. This takes around 20 seconds.

Serve immediately.

SALMON AVOCADO LUNCH

Ingredients:

4 ounces of cold salmon (wild sockeye), smoked

A Hass avocado

Sea salt to taste

Instructions:

Slice the salmon and make them into four pieces and the avocado into about 4-inch pieces.

Cover the pieces of avocado with the salmon pieces and add salt.

Serve and enjoy.

PORK SHOULDERS & BRUSSEL SPROUTS

Ingredients:

Brussels sprouts:

A pound of halved brussels sprouts

2 teaspoons of ground turmeric

2 tablespoons of unsalted butter, grass-fed

2 teaspoons of sea salt

Pork Shoulders:

6 strips of pastured, uncooked bacon (high-quality)

4 lbs. of pastured pork shoulder

3 teaspoons of ground turmeric

2 tablespoons of dried oregano

Half cup of apple cider vinegar (optional)

Half cup of xylitol (optional)

Sea salt

Instructions:

Put the bacon strips on a slow cooker, at its base. Put some turmeric, salt, and oregano on the pork and put it on top of the bacon strips.

Cook them on low fire for 14-16 hours. Shred the meat by using a fork. (For an added tangy sweet-and-sour barbecue flavor, mix the drippings from slow cooker with apple cider vinegar and xylitol and put them in a pan. Cook on low heat and let it simmer for about 5 minutes. This can be used as your sauce)

For your sprouts, preheat oven to 300ºF. Put the Brussel sprouts in a pan used for baking, and put salt, butter, and turmeric around it. Cook and bake for 30-45 minutes.

Roasted Rack of Lamb and Fennel, Celery, and Cauliflower

Ingredients:

A rack of organic lamb (American), grass-fed, about 1 and 1/2 pounds or 8 chops

A tablespoon each of freshly chopped thyme, sage, turmeric, oregano, and rosemary

A tablespoon of ghee

2 cups of sliced fennel

Sea salt to taste

2 cups of sliced cauliflower

2 cups of sliced celery

Instructions:

Heat the oven to 350ºF.

Put ghee all over the lamb and diagonally score the top fat.

Add the salt and put the chopped herbs over the lamb.

Put the vegetables in the pan, and put the lamb on top, make sure the fat-side is facing up.

Let it bake for about 45 minutes or until it goes up to 125 degrees in the thickest side of the lamb. Put in the oven over low heat, and cook for 3 more minutes to make the skin crispy.

Fish and Butternut Squash

Ingredients:

Squash preparations:

A medium-sized butternut squash (seeded and peeled, chopped into 1" cubes)

4 tablespoons of unsalted butter, grass-fed

4 medium-sized peeled carrots (chopped into 1" pieces)

Half tablespoon of vinegar, apple cider

A spring onion (chopped into 4 slices)

Sea salt

2-3 tablespoons of MCT oil

Fish preparations:

A pound of tilapia filets

1/4 cup of ground coffee beans

A tablespoon of dried oregano

1/4 teaspoon of vanilla powder

3 tablespoons of xylitol

2 tablespoons of sea salt

A tablespoon of ground turmeric

Instructions:

Heat the oven up 320 degrees F.

Mix the vanilla powder, coffee beans, turmeric, xylitol, salt, and oregano in a container. Pour over fish generously and rub the mixture in.

Put the fish in a dish used for baking (single-layer).

Put the dish on the middle rack inside the oven. You should bake it for about 8-10 minutes or until it is properly cooked.

Steam the carrots and squash until tender.

Put it in the blender along with the remaining ingredients, blend to reach the consistency desired.

BOWL OF BERRIES

Ingredients:

Half cup of raspberries

Half cup of blueberries

Half cup of strawberries

Juice from half a lemon

1/4 cup of fresh basil, chopped

Instructions:

Remove the stems of the berries and chop them up.

In a container, stir together the lemon juice and the berries.

Top them with basil that are chopped and it is ready for serving!

BONE BROTH RECIPE

Ingredients:

Any leftover bones of chicken, pork or beef, except fish

Apple cider vinegar

Water

Onions, peeled and chopped

Parsley or celery greens and other herbs and spices of your choice

Instructions:

Roast the leftover bones the night before for more texture.

Put water in a pot and add the bones. Make sure the water covers the bones.

Add the apple cider vinegar.

Bring it to a boil and leave to simmer.

Skim the impurities and keep simmering.

Once you see no scum on the surface, keep simmering, adding water to cover the bones.

Prepare your veggies and herbs and spices.

For chicken: simmer for 15 to 18 hours then add your veggies and herbs and spices. For beef: simmer for 35 to 40 hours then add veggies and herbs and spices. Add the celery greens or parsley only at the last hour of simmering.

Add more veggies as desired and no need to add more water.

Simmer for another hour or two and it's done.

CHOCOLATE PUDDING

Ingredients:

4 tablespoons of hardwood xylitol or stevia

4 cups of divided coconut milk that is BpA-free

2 tablespoons of vanilla powder

A tablespoon of gelatin, grass-fed

A tablespoon of MCT oil

3/4 cup of chocolate powder

1/4 cup of macadamia nuts

4 tablespoons of butter, unsalted

Instructions:

Heat a cup of the coconut milk, the stevia, and the gelatin in the pan. Do this over medium heat until they all dissolve.

Put the remaining three cups of coconut milk in a food processor or blender with the chocolate powder, vanilla, oil, and butter then blend.

Add the mixture of coconut milk and gelatin to your blender. Blend until combined. Adding macadamia nuts is optional.

Put the blender contents into ramekins or muffin tins and store in the refrigerator for 1 hour.

Top it with nuts (optional).

CHICKEN HERB PREPARED WITH CREAM SAUCE

This is a delicious meal that you can have for supper and even have the leftovers for lunch the following day. This meal can make four servings.

Ingredients

Chicken broth, ½ cup

Dried tarragon, 1 teaspoon

Butter, divided into 5 tablespoons

Salt to taste

Dry white wine, ½ cup

Raw chicken breasts, 4 pieces

Heavy cream, ½ cup

Dried tarragon, 1 teaspoon

Garlic cloves, 3 pieces

8 oz of cream cheese

Small white onions (thinly sliced), 2 pieces

Herbes De Provence, 1 ½ teaspoon

Canadian chicken seasoning, 1 teaspoon

Instructions

Use 2 tablespoons of butter to sauté the garlic, tarragon and onions in a skillet over medium heat. When they become soft, remove them from the skillet and keep them aside.

Put about 2 tablespoons of butter in the skillet you have used before placing it on low heat. Let it melt before adding the wine. You can then add cream cheese and stir until it melts and mixes with the butter and wine. Continue adding spices and cream while stirring until it is properly mixed.

You can preheat your oven up to about 350°. F. Grease the 9/13 glass baking dish using a tablespoon of butter before putting the chicken broth inside it.

Make sure you put chicken on the baking dish. You can do it in one layer.

Spread the mixture over the chicken using a spoon and make sure you do it evenly.

Using a spoon, spread the cream sauce mixture too on the onions and chicken. Let it bake for about 45 minutes to one hour.

Your meal is now ready and you can serve it with a salad.

Low Carb Egg Salad

This recipe gives you an opportunity to prepare an egg salad but with an amazing twist. You can add butter in order for it to have great flavor. This can make three servings.

Ingredients

Ground mustard, ½

Finely minced white onion, ½ cup

Melted butter, 2 tablespoons

Black pepper, 1 teaspoon

Mayonnaise, ½ cup

Salt, I teaspoon

Instructions

Take a large pot and fill it with water before putting in the eggs. Let it boil and leave it to cook for about 10 minutes.

After the 10 minutes, you can remove the pot from the heat and try to pour out all the hot water you are able to. Let the eggs remain in the pot and replace the hot water with cold water.

Leave the eggs in the cold water for about 2-3 minutes before removing, patting them dry and then proceeding to peel them.

Now that you have your peeled eggs, you should chop them into uniform pieces each taking about ¼ inch. You can use an egg slicer to make your work easier.

You can add the rest of the ingredients and mix properly. Store it in the fridge until when you are ready to eat it.

Spinach Salad Recipe

Although you can prepare the basic salad, you can also make it tastier and different by adding various types of cheese, onions and nuts. Feta, blue cheese and gorgonzola work best. Spinach has lots of vitamins K, A and also potassium magnesium and is great especially when you are following the Ketogenic diet.

Ingredients for preparing the Basic Spinach Salad

Cooked and crumbled bacon, about ½ cup

Baby spinach leaves, 3-4 cups (they should be washed)

Slivered almonds, ¼ (alternatively, you can go for chopped macadamia nuts)

Thinly sliced red onion, ½ cup

Crumbled blue cheese, 3- 4 tablespoons

Instructions

Split the spinach leaves into four salad plates

You can then lay the onion over the spinach

Take the nuts, bacon crumbles and cheese and sprinkle them on the onion and spinach

Spoon on any low carb dressing you prefer and an example is Feta Vinagrette

Ingredients for preparing Spinach and Apple Salad

Crumbled blue cheese, about 3-4 tablespoons

Baby spinach leaves, 3-4 cups (they should be washed)

Thinly sliced red onion, ½ cup

½ small apple. You should cut them to form ¼ inch cubes

Instructions

Split the spinach leaves into four salad plates

You can then lay the onion over the spinach

Take the apple and sprinkle it on the onion and spinach

Spoon on any low carb dressing you prefer and an example is Feta Vinagrette

BEEF BURGUNDY RECIPE

Ingredients:

3 lbs. of beef cut into cubes for about 2 inches each

1/4 lb. of bacon

4 tablespoons of butter

1/4 tablespoon of pepper

1 and a half tablespoons of salt

2 sliced carrots

2 tablespoons of almond flour

A tablespoon of tomato paste

A sliced onion

A tablespoon of thyme (fresh or dried)

2 cloves garlic, finely chopped

3 cups of full-bodied red wine such as Cotes du Rhone or Chianti

A tablespoon of fresh parsley, finely chopped

A bay leaf

A lb. of white or brown crimini mushrooms

2 1/2 cups beef stock

Instructions:

Preheat your oven to 425.

Prepare the bacon by cutting them into short strips. You can sauté the bacon in a deep saucepan using a tablespoon of butter. Let the bacon cook properly, making sure it is not crispy.

Use a paper towel to pat dry the beef. Add the beef into the bacon in 3 to 4 batches. Make sure to cook until each batch of meat is brown before removing from pan.

Put the meat and bacon aside in a casserole baking dish. You will be using this in the oven later on. Add the pepper, salt, and almond flour over the meat in an even manner.

Cook the meat by baking it in the oven for 10 minutes and do not put a cover on it. In this way, the flour is absorbed into the meat and might make a slight crust.

Take it from the oven and lower the heat to 325.

Mix a tablespoon of butter with the remaining fat from the bacon and meat in the saucepan. It is time to sauté the onion and carrots for 8 minutes or until soft.

Add the garlic, tomato paste, bay leaf, thyme, and parsley.

Mix in the beef broth and wine. Bring this to a boil and let it simmer for about 3 to 5 minutes. Put the meat on a casserole pan and pour in the mixture.

Put the lid on the dish. Bake in the oven for about 2 and a half hours. The meat should be done if you can pull it apart with a fork.

You should sautee the mushrooms and remaining butter in a pan while the meat is cooking.

Once the meat is cooked, take the casserole pan from the oven.

Drain the liquid from the pan using a colander.

Bring the liquid to a boil and simmer for 8 to 10 minutes. Pour over meat and mushrooms. Garnish with parsley and serve.

CHOCOLATE PEANUT BUTTER ICE CREAM

Ingredients:

¾ cup and 2 tablespoons of coconut oil

4 tablespoons of skinny fat MCT oil

Half cup of water or unsweetened almond milk

4 egg yolks

4 whole eggs

A vanilla bean or 2 teaspoons of vanilla

1/4 cup of Swerve confectioners or 1 teaspoon of stevia glyceride

Half teaspoon of salt

¼ cup of unsweetened cocoa powder

PEANUT BUTTER SWIRL:

Half cup of natural peanut butter

¼ cup of melted coconut oil

¼ cup of swerve confectioners or 1 tsp stevia according to your taste

Instructions:

Using a blender or food processor, put in the MCT oil, coconut oil, eggs, water or almond milk, yolks, natural sweetener, vanilla bean seeds, cocoa powder, and salt.

Blend the ingredients until the mixture is smooth. Pour them into the ice cream maker turn it on.

While the ice cream is getting ready, get started on the peanut butter swirl. Combine the natural sweetener, peanut butter, and coconut oil/butter in a small container.

Mix the ingredients until they become smooth. Keep in the fridge to stay cool while waiting for the ice cream.

Swirl the mixture into the ice cream maker during the last half a minute.

Turn the ice cream maker off and put the contents in a container that's airtight before placing in the freezer.

CREAMY COCONUT ICE CREAM

Ingredients:

2 teaspoon of vanilla

3 tablespoon + 2 teaspoon/50 g MCT oil

4 yolks aside from the whole eggs

4 pastured whole eggs

A tablespoon/80-160 g of erythritol or xylitol

1 gram of vitamin C/ascorbic acid (you can also use lime juice or apple cider vinegar, 10 drops)

Half cup/100g of water or ice

7 tablespoons/100g of coconut oil

7 tablespoons/100g of butter, grass-fed

1/4 to half cup of upgraded chocolate powder (low-toxin), optional

Instructions:

Mix all ingredients in the blender except the water or ice. You need to make sure the mixture reaches a creamy texture before adding in the water.

Pour in water or the ice and continue blending until fully incorporated. The ideal consistency is of that of a yogurt or ice cream.

Put the mix into the ice cream maker. Turn on the ice cream maker.

Taco Salad Recipe

Ingredients:

The Salad prep:

A quarter cup of red cabbage, shredded

Half of an avocado cut into slices

A cup of spring lettuce

A cucumber, sliced

2 carrots, shredded

The Taco Mix prep:

Half of freshly squeezed lime

A pound of fatty ground beef, organic and grass-fed

A teaspoon of dried oregano

A tablespoon of cayenne powder

2 tablespoons of unsalted butter, grass-fed or ghee

Sea salt

The Avocado Dressing prep:

A quarter cup of apple cider vinegar

A quarter cup of MCT oil

A cup of fresh cilantro, chopped

A quarter cup of fresh lemon juice

2 avocados

4 cups of cucumber, sliced

Sea salt

4 spring onions

Instructions:

Using a medium-sized pan, cook beef thoroughly and sauté until cooked. Remove the excess fat from the pan and put in the cayenne powder, ghee or butter, oregano, salt, and lime juice. Take it away from the fire and just set it aside.

Combine the ingredients from the salad and put them into plates. Top them off with the beef mix.

Pour the ingredients of the dressing into the blender and mix until creamy and smooth. Drizzle the mixture on top of the salad.

THE SHEPHERD'S PIE

Ingredients:

THE FILLING PREP:

Half cup of frozen peas

A tablespoon of dried parsley

A pound of ground beef or lamb (grass-fed), can also be a combination of the two

A teaspoon of dried rosemary

A medium-sized onion

A clove of garlic

1 and 1/2 tablespoons of tomato paste

2 carrots

2 tablespoons of butter (grass-fed), beef tallow (grass-fed), or hog lard (pastured)

2 celery stalks

Sea salt

Salt and pepper

THE MASHED TOPPING PREP:

Your choice of: 1 and 1/2 pounds of potatoes, 1 and 1/2 pounds of root vegetables of your choice (must be mashable), A head of cauliflower, or 1 and 1/2 pounds of sweet potatoes

1/4 cup of coconut milk (full-fat) or heavy cream

A tablespoon of ghee or grass-fed butter

Salt and pepper to taste

Instructions:

Using a saucepan, boil the chopped cauliflower, potatoes, or your root vegetables. Once done, drain the water and add the remaining ingredients of the mashed topping prep and start mashing.

Preheat your oven up to 350 degrees.

Clean and chop the onion, garlic, celery, and carrots. In a heavy pan, sauté the tallow, lard, or butter adding a pinch of salt. Once cooked, put the tomato paste, peas, and other spices.

Make a space in the middle of the heavy pan. Cook the ground lamb or beef adding salt. Break them up to pieces.

Put the mixture into separate oven-safe plates or containers and add mashed potatoes and/or veggies on top. Cook by baking for 20 to 30 minutes.

Squash Soup with Butternut and Red Thai Curry

Ingredients:

A clove of garlic (minced)

1 to 2 tablespoons of butter, coconut oil, tallow, or lard

3/4 cup of coconut milk (full fat)

Sea salt

3 cups of beef or chicken broth

Squash and curry paste mixture:

A teaspoon of cumin

A teaspoon of fresh ginger (chopped)

A teaspoon of coriander

Juice from a lime

A tablespoon of fish sauce

1 to 2 shallots

2 cloves of garlic

2 stalks of lemongrass, fresh (chopped)

2 to 4 red chilies, remove seeds

9 cups of butternut squash (peeled and cubed)

2 tablespoons of chopped cilantro leaves (optional)

Instructions:

Cut the butternut squash in half and remove the seeds. Put it in a cookie sheet and bake in the oven with a little water at 350 degrees. Bake for around half an hour.

Using a big soup pot, sauté the garlic in the fat of your choice and add a sprinkle of salt to taste. Wait until soft.

Pour the broth with the coconut milk in the pot and let it simmer on low fire. You can prepare the curry paste mixture while the broth is simmering.

Mix all of the ingredients of the curry paste, except the squash, and put them in the blender or a food processor and mix until paste-like.

Get the squash from its shells and put in around 1/4 of it into the blender. Do this one piece at a time while continuously blending with the paste. Do this until all of the squash and the mix are blended.

Pour in the curry or squash paste mix to the pot and stir to mix. Let the mixture simmer for a few more minutes. You can make your main dish or salad afterwards.

ROSEMARY & BACON WITH SAUTÉED RADISHES

Ingredients:

2 bunches of radishes, sliced in halves and removed stems

A tablespoon of rosemary, chopped

5 oz. of chopped bacon, slices of half-inch thick

Salt & pepper

2 peeled garlic cloves

Balsamic vinegar for finishing, optional

Instructions:

Cook the bacon in a medium-sized pan on medium heat. Stir often to make sure the fat is cooked and the bacon turns crispy. Remove the bacon and make sure you leave the fat in the pan.

Put in the radishes and turn the heat into medium high. Add salt and pepper and cook for about 3 to 4 minutes. Keep cooking and start tossing the radishes. Put some rosemary and cook for 8 to 10 minutes more. To make sure they are cooked and not burned, alternate the heat from medium to medium high. Test the radishes with a fork.

Bring down the heat to medium; add the garlic cloves on top of the radishes. Give it another toss and cook for another minute. Serve with a dash of balsamic vinegar.

CRUSTLESS QUICHE

Ingredients:

12 whole eggs

2 cups of chopped greens (fresh lacinato kale, spinach, broccoli)

4 to 6 pieces of bacon (pastured), you can also use pork sausage

1 teaspoon of coconut oil

Black pepper, ground

Sea salt

Instructions:

Cut the bacon in small slices and partially cook. If you're using the sausage, cook beforehand.

Put the greens in and put a lid on it to make the cooking faster and to avoid drying. You can also add the pepper while softening the veggies.

Preheat your oven at 350 degrees.

Whisk the eggs in a medium-sized bowl.

Put coconut oil into a pie pan and mix in the whisked eggs.

Pour in the vegetable mix on top of the eggs.

Put the pie pan in the oven and bake for about 30 to 35 minutes.

Remove the pie pan and let it cool. Cut the pie in a few pieces and enjoy!

Golden Rod Egg (Paleo-friendly)

Ingredients:

6 pieces of hard-boiled eggs

1/8 teaspoon of pepper

2 tablespoons of your choice of fat (ghee, unsalted grass-fed butter, lard, or bacon fat)

3/8 teaspoon of salt, you can cut down if you use bacon fat

A cup of milk of your choice

A tablespoon of arrowroot powder

Instructions:

Remove the egg peelings of the boiled egg and separate the yolks from the whites. Use an egg slicer to cut the whites and use a fork to mash the yolks.

Heat the butter or your fat of choice in a pan and add the arrowroot powder with some salt and pepper. Cook it on low heat. This would make the white sauce.

Constantly stir and add in the milk you chose. Cook until the sauce is thick, over low-medium heat.

Put the egg whites in the mixture.

Spread the mashed egg yolk on top of the mixture and serve.

SPICED PUMPKIN LATTE

Ingredients:

2 cups of brewed coffee (dark), you can also use an espresso

3/4 cup of coconut milk

3/4 cup of almond milk

1 tsp. of pumpkin pie spice

1/3 cup of maple syrup (Grade B)

Half tsp. of vanilla extract

3 tbsp. of pumpkin puree

Instructions:

In a saucepan, put all the ingredients and cook over medium-high heat. Let it simmer for about 5 minutes. Whisk it occasionally. Wait until thoroughly heated and frothy on top.

Transfer the liquid mix into your blender and use a towel to cover on top. Mix and blend for 30 minutes (high). Wait until it is foamy on top.

Pour into mugs and serve.

DRIED FIGS WRAPPED IN PROSCIUTTO WITH WALNUTS

Ingredients:

9 sliced and halved lengthwise, pieces of prosciutto

18 dried figs

18 pieces of toothpicks

18 dried walnuts, halved or quartered

Instructions:

Chop the stems off of the figs. Make the incision into the fig from the end that was cut.

Put the walnuts that were halved or quartered into the figs.

Put and wrap the prosciutto on each fig and put a toothpick through it all the way to the other side.

You can also opt to bake or cook the figs if you don't want cold ones.

BREAKFAST BREAD

Ingredients:

Half cup of roasted almond butter

¼ tsp. of sea salt (celtic)

2 pieces of large eggs

¼ tsp. of stevia

¼ tsp. of baking soda

A tsp. of vanilla extract

A tbsp. of ground cinnamon

Instructions:

Pour in the almond butter in a big bowl and mix until creamy.

Add in the eggs, stevia, and vanilla.

Put the cinnamon, baking soda and salt.

Combine well with the hand blender until the ingredients are fully mixed.

Put the batter in a greased 8x8" baking dish

Bake for 12-15 minutes at 325 degrees.

Serve and enjoy.

Squeak and Bubble Cakes

Ingredients:

2 to 3 carrots (they should be chopped and peeled)

A celery root, chopped and peeled

A Yukon of gold potato, chopped and peeled

A large parsnip, chopped and peeled

A celery root, chopped and peeled

Half of a savoy cabbage, sliced

A leek, sliced

A handful sliced kale

Salt

A tablespoon of butter

A tablespoon of olive oil

2 pieces of farm eggs

Ground black pepper

A handful of chopped parsley

Instructions:

Put the parsnip, carrots, celery root, and potato in a big pan of boiling water with salt. Cook these ingredients until they are very soft. This may take about 20 to 25 minutes. Remove the water and put them back in the pan.

Mash the veggies together roughly.

Melt 1/2 of the butter in the frying pan and cook the leek for about 4 to 5 minutes to soften it. Add in the cabbage and kale, sauté until warmed for a bit. Pour it into the mashed veggies and season black pepper and salt.

Separate the mix into 4 and using your hands, make them into patties. You can then store in the fridge for about 30 to 45 minutes.

When the patties are cold, melt a tablespoon of olive oil and butter in a pan. Put the cakes in the pan and cook until crispy and golden, flip to the other side. Once both sides are crisp, put them lined up on your tray and put it in the oven at 350 degrees.

Cook the eggs and add salt and pepper to taste. Put them on top of the cakes with chopped parsley before serving.

THE KETOGENIC CACAO

Ingredients:

Half cup of coconut milk, full-fat

Half cup of water

2 tablespoons of unsalted Kerrygold butter/any pastured butter

1/4 teaspoon of vanilla extract

2 tablespoons of regular or raw cacao powder

Cinnamon

Instructions:

Mix the coconut milk and water and bring to a boil in a saucepan.

Combine the boiling mix with the other ingredients and put them in a mixing bowl.

Mix in a blender or hand mixer, wait until frothy.

Pour into a mug and serve!

Avocado Baked Eggs

Ingredients:

An avocado

2 small eggs

Salt and pepper to taste

Instructions:

Put aluminum foil in a baking sheet.

Slice the avocado in half and take out the pit. Put them on the aluminum foil.

Crack the eggs and fit them in the avocado pits. You might need to scrape off some avocado to make room for the eggs. Make sure the avocados are balanced so they can hold the eggs in their position.

Put the avocados in the oven and bake for about 15 to 20 minutes.

Add salt and pepper as desired and enjoy!

Cauliflower and Sweet Potato Soup

Ingredients:

A large head of cauliflower

3 medium-large sized sweet potatoes, peeled and cut into inch slices

A sweet diced onion

2 cloves of garlic

7 cups of water, filtered

Instructions:

Cut the cauliflower into pieces that are easy to eat and preheat your oven at 400 degrees F.

Put the cauliflower on a cookie sheet and lightly drizzle it with olive oil. Put it in the oven and cook until lightly brown and soft. This might take 20 minutes to half an hour.

In a large pot, mix the onion, sweet potato, garlic, and water and let it boil. Add salt and stir. Let it simmer on low until the sweet potatoes are tender.

Divide into two parts, blending one part then adding it on top of the other afterwards. Enjoy!

CONCLUSION

For every person who wants to eat healthy and live longer, these recipes are the best ones to make. You can share these with your family and friends and have a fit and healthy mind and body. Staying healthy is a good thing and it's not always hard to do. Get rid of your perceptions about crash-dieting and starving yourself to lose a few pounds, you can still enjoy eating while losing weight.

Make sure you are equipped with the right knowledge and the right approaches to having a balanced diet and a healthier physique. These recipes will surely be your key to achieving the body you've always wanted and you've always needed.

Thank you again for downloading this book!

I hope this book was able to help you to *Easy Recipes to Lose up to 1 Pound a Day! Simple & Delicious Meals for Healthy Weight Loss, Paleo Friendly*

Finally, if you enjoyed this book, then I'd like to ask you for a favor, would you be kind enough to leave a review for this book on Amazon? It'd be greatly appreciated!

Click here to leave a review for this book on Amazon!

Thank you and good luck!

Amanda

Printed in Great Britain
by Amazon